Student Leadership Training

A WORKBOOK TO REINFORCE EFFECTIVE COMMUNICATION SKILLS

Diane Taub

A SCARECROWEDUCATION BOOK
The Scarecrow Press, Inc.
Lanham, Maryland, and Oxford
2002

A SCARECROWEDUCATION BOOK

Published in the United States of America
by Scarecrow Press, Inc.
A Member of the Rowman & Littlefield Publishing Group
4720 Boston Way, Lanham, Maryland 20706
www.scarecroweducation.com

PO Box 317
Oxford
OX2 9RU, UK

British Library Cataloguing in Publication Information Available

Library of Congress Cataloging-in-Publication Data

Taub, Diane, 1949–
  Student leadership training : a workbook to reinforce effective communication skills / Diane Taub.
    p. cm.
"A Scarecrow Education book."
Includes bibliographical references.
  ISBN 0-8108-4555-5 (pbk. : alk. paper)
 1. Communication in education—United States. 2. Leadership—Study and teaching—United States.
3. Students—United States—Life skills guides. I. Title.
LB1033.5 .T38 2002
371.4'047—dc21   2002012261

CONTENTS

GROUP DYNAMICS   3

In order to build a more cohesive group, guidelines for effective training are discussed in this section. When participants feel comfortable within a group, the basic communication skills can be learned more easily. This is the cornerstone for becoming a peer leader.

NONVERBAL COMMUNICATION   11

The communication process includes nonverbal as well as verbal expression. This chapter examines how behavior expresses meaning more clearly than words. To be an effective peer leader, one must consider not only words but also body language and tone of voice when attempting to comprehend the message someone is trying to convey.

ROADBLOCKS   17

Roadblocks are responses we usually say unintentionally that impede effective communication. They show lack of respect and create distrust. The main objective of this section is to raise awareness of how roadblocks can hinder effective communication.

LISTENING   27

Listening is an integral part of everyday life often taken for granted. It is a valuable skill in becoming a peer leader. If listening skills are well developed they can be powerful tools for successful communication. This section attempts to explain how effective listeners work to understand, accept, and respond to both the meaning and the feelings of the person speaking.

QUESTIONING   37

In this section, learning how to ask effective questions is explored. Questioning is a skill that takes practice and considerable effort to master. Effective questioning can help to maintain open lines of communication, just as ineffective questioning can prohibit communication from developing into a more meaningful conversation.

FOREWORD

The practice of students helping each other achieve their goals and dreams has a long historical tradition. Tutoring, for example, has ancient origins and remains one of the most powerful ways that students learn from each other. Student leadership has a more recent beginning yet is equally as widespread in schools across North America. But the most profound example of students helping each other and one that has the most power for creating a safe and peaceful world is when students actively demonstrate their care for one another.

Typically called **peer helping** or **peer assistance**, this method of students helping other students is based on their natural willingness and desire to talk to someone who will listen and understand, is nonjudgmental and accepting, and in many cases has had similar life experiences. What I discovered thirty years ago when I first started in this field is still true today: young people, when experiencing a worry, frustration, or problem, are more likely to seek the counsel of another young person than to discuss the issue with an adult.

Why not help young people have better skills to help their friends? Why not provide them with the training and supervision to turn peer pressure into peer support? Through our research we learned many years ago that not only was this possible, but that young people could easily take responsibility for exceptional leadership in this field.

But youths cannot do this completely on their own. They need the support and assistance of highly skilled and caring professionals who can be role models. At the same time, these adult professionals must know how to nurture the abilities of youth without taking over or "professionalizing" what young people can do for and with each other.

One of those adult leaders is Diane Taub, whom I have had the pleasure to work with for many years. While we first met when she was a participant in my peer training leadership workshop, she has since become one of the top peer trainers in North America and has learned quite clearly how to assist students to demonstrate their caring, creativity, and responsibility. The student team that produced this workbook under Diane Taub's supervision truly understood not only what it takes to learn the skills and attitudes necessary to be an effective student leader, but also how to put those skills and attitudes into practice.

This student workbook is designed to follow the training sessions that appear in our leader's guide, *The Peer Helping Starter Kit*, available from Peer Resources at

www.peer.ca/peer.html or by calling 1-800-567-3700. However, the thoroughness of the workbook enables it to match up with many other training guides available. Most importantly, this workbook will benefit any student leadership program where students want to put their caring for each other into practice.

Our nonprofit organization has developed a reputation as a global authority on peer leadership and we pledge our assistance to anyone using this workbook. We know that the future of our world depends on the skills, determination, and caring of our youth. We hope that this workbook will provide students across North America with the navigation tools to make their dreams and goals come true.

Rey A. Carr, Ph.D.
Chief Executive Officer
Peer Resources
ceo@peer.ca

PREFACE

I have seen over the many years of my work with teenagers, students, and adults that the best way to learn is from each other. We all learn from our peers.

This workbook has been thirty years in the making. As far as I know, it is the first of its kind written with input from students themselves. It is for, by, and about teenagers communicating with teenagers.

It is not a be-all and end-all, but one more tool in the practice and success of student leadership programs of any kind; a companion to a variety of resources already written on these kinds of programs.

This workbook is the product of a small group of students from Harvard-Westlake, an extraordinary school—one of the most renowned private schools in Los Angeles, indeed in the country—with which I am associated. While their emphasis is still on academic excellence and individual achievement, social skills and personal interactions dealing with life's challenges now take their rightful place alongside academics.

The idea came to me when the students in my class said they wanted to update the workbook they had been using to make it more meaningful to them. They felt it didn't really speak to them or address their needs.

Over the course of a summer we volunteered our time and devoted our attention to creating the workbook that follows.

We then spent a semester using it ourselves, in our classes, working out the kinks, honing it, and weeding out what worked and what didn't work. This is what we are left with.

We hope you find it as helpful as we do. We had the added benefit of learning by doing. The result was a task we will never forget and will forever be grateful for.

ACKNOWLEDGMENTS

To Harvard-Westlake's Senior Peer Support Leaders Gabriela Helfet, Alexis Johnson, Andrew Herr, Marisa Schwab, Noel Hyun, and Andrew Lee who worked tirelessly to help create our vision. Your dedication and commitment to peer support, your constant enthusiasm, and your wonderful words of wisdom will forever inspire me.

And to all my trainees, leaders, and tutors at Harvard-Westlake School, and to all the students, mentors, and benefactors I have had over the thirty years of my teaching, both in Canada and the United States, I say, "Thank you!"

I have gained more from them than they can ever imagine. And I hope that I have affected them in some small way to help repay what they've given to me and how they have enriched my life.

I'd also like to acknowledge Rey Carr, who has been my mentor, my role model, and a very special friend. He inspired me to believe in myself and my abilities to impact others, which enabled me to use my passion for peer support in so many ways. Certainly this workbook could not have happened without his encouragement, his ideas, and his invaluable feedback.

To my children Allison and Josh, who have certainly helped me immeasurably to communicate more effectively as they have grown into sensitive, loving, and extraordinary young adults.

And a very special thank-you to my husband, Bill, who is my greatest supporter. His unconditional love, patience, and wonderful suggestions helped me see this project to fruition.

INTRODUCTION

"You give but little when you give of your possessions.
It is when you give of yourself that you truly give."
—Kahlil Gibran

When several of my high school seniors approached me with their concern that the basic communication skills that were being reinforced did not reflect their daily experiences, I suggested that they help me write a comprehensive workbook that clearly and concisely outlines the skills necessary to be effective communicators. Using examples from their perspectives and experiences will be beneficial in making the training more appropriate for the specific needs of our program. It is a common misconception that speaking a language automatically allows one to communicate effectively. However, effective communication requires awareness of the skills in this workbook and their proper application. These skills and techniques are simply one way to be effective in communicating with their peers.

To help reinforce these communication skills, I have used the process of the Experiential Learning Cycle (ELC), as developed by Carr, deRosenroll, and Saunders (1992). The ELC has been tremendously effective in the student leadership training. Therefore, I have made a point to incorporate this process into our workbook. It has helped students maximize each activity by reflecting on their own personal experiences and has encouraged them to apply what they have learned about themselves in their daily lives. In every section of the workbook, the ELC plays a key role in the debrief. After the classroom debrief, you will notice a page entitled "Personal Thoughts and Notes." The purpose of this page is for each trainee to take the opportunity to reflect on each personal experience. Over the years, it has become clear to me that often some people have difficulties verbalizing their feelings in front of the classroom. This page gives students the opportunity to process the experience through writing, in addition to the group discussion.

Writing this workbook has been an enlightening experience for all of us. I hope you will reap the benefits of our labor of love.

GROUP DYNAMICS

Student Leadership Training

GROUP DYNAMICS

Guidelines for an Effective Training Group

In order to feel comfortable within a group so that basic communication skills can be learned, one must take the following into consideration:

1. **Trust.** Trust enables you to express your feelings without reservations by knowing that the group members will be supportive.
2. **Confidentiality.** Confidentiality ensures privacy and subsequently a sense of comfort knowing that what is being shared within the group remains in the group.
3. **Honesty and Openness.** Through being open and honest with your feelings and experiences, personal growth and the opportunity to learn from others within the group can be achieved.
4. **Open-mindedness.** Knowing that others within the group are open-minded, one can feel comfortable to take risks and disclose personal information without fear of judgment.
5. **Tolerance.** Tolerance allows for recognition and acceptance of differences within the group, thus ensuring a safer and more open environment.
6. **Respect.** Respect gives everyone the time and attention they deserve to fully express their opinions without interruption.
7. **Safety.** Safety allows for a secure environment in which participants will not be physically or emotionally harmed in any way.
8. **Attentiveness.** Paying attention when a person speaks allows for that person to feel that their opinions are accepted and heard.

Before we move on to the activity, we would like to highlight the two key elements that enhance the success of an effective training group.

Trust

As a leader, how can you build trust with others?

1. Make commitments as a student leader. Making and maintaining your prior arrangements is important. When you make commitments you show that you want to spend time with that person.
2. Be punctual. This makes you a physically reliable person because it shows that you value your time spent with others.
3. Understand the individual. Trying to grasp what others are feeling gives them a sense that you are concerned and interested in what they are saying.
4. Show personal integrity. Staying true to your beliefs helps others regard you as dependable and reliable.
5. Pay attention to details. This enables the speaker to feel appreciated and valued.
6. Clarify expectations. It is important to make sure everyone knows and understands what it takes to create a safe environment in order to gain everyone's trust.

Confidentiality

One of the key aspects needed to maintain a strong, cohesive bond within a peer support group is confidentiality. It is important to develop a sense of trust through confidentiality in order to ensure group success. Confidentiality means keeping personal information that is shared with you during training to yourself. However, there is one exception to the issue of confidentiality. That is, if someone brings up any one of a number of **red flag issues**.

In order to ensure the safety of our peers, it is our school policy, as well as our moral and ethical commitment, to report any red flag issues to our program coordinator. The following are red flag issues:

- If a member is hurting themselves (i.e., suicide threats, eating disorders)
- If a member is hurting someone else (i.e., abuse, harassment)
- If someone is hurting a member (i.e., abuse, harassment)

Following these guidelines to ensure the safety of your peers is of utmost importance.

Group Dynamics Activity 1

Goals

1. To build a more cohesive group
2. To learn more about each other

Directions

Find a partner in your class whom you don't know very well. Spend the next ten minutes getting acquainted with your partner by asking the following questions. Remember to take notes.

1. Share a special quality about yourself. Explain how this quality is special.

2. Describe an activity you enjoy most in your spare time and why you enjoy this activity.

3. Describe a place you enjoy going to and why you enjoy going there.

4. If you received a "good news" phone call, what would it be?

5. Who is or was the most significant person in your life? How has this person had an impact on you?

6. Relate a meaningful experience in your life.

In small groups

Once the interviews are over, form into small groups of eight to ten people. Have each partnership introduce themselves to the small group starting with a positive impression of the person interviewed. Every member of the group will continue to introduce their partner with the information they learned about each other.

Debrief

Observations. I noticed that . . .

1. What did you notice while your partner was introducing you to the group?
2. How did your partner respond to the way you introduced him/her to the group? (verbal or nonverbal)
3. What were some of the similarities and/or differences that you noticed during the introductions?

Personal meaning. I realized or learned or it was reconfirmed for me that . . .

1. What made it comfortable/uncomfortable for you to be introduced to the class?
2. How well do you need to know a person to disclose personal information?

Action plan. How can you apply what you realized or learned about yourself in another situation? In the future I will . . .

1. How will your level of trust within the group change?
2. What might you do differently in future interactions with your peers?
3. How does trust impact your relations with peers?

Personal Thoughts and Notes

Observations. I noticed that . . .

Personal meaning. I learned or realized or it was reconfirmed for me that . . .

Action plan. How can you apply what you realized or learned about yourself in another situation? In the future I will . . .

NONVERBAL
COMMUNICATION

Student Leadership Training

NONVERBAL COMMUNICATION

The communication process includes nonverbal expression as well as verbal expression. Sometimes behavior expresses meaning more clearly than words do.

To be an effective peer leader one must consider not only words but also body language and tone of voice when attempting to comprehend the message that someone is trying to convey.

Some studies have shown that body language and tone of voice are more important than words in communicating. Therefore, peer leaders should pay very close attention to the nonverbal cues since sometimes they convey more crucial information than just the words being said.

An effective method for remembering nonverbal communication skills is the acronym FELOR.

Face the person

Eye contact

Lean toward the person

Open posture

Relax

Face the person. It is very difficult to sustain a meaningful and effective conversation without facing the person squarely. Not only keep your face toward them, but also keep your body positioned toward him or her at all times. This tells people that you are interested in what they have to say.

Eye contact. Without eye contact, the person may think that you are uninterested. It can dissuade the person you are talking to from truly opening up. Therefore, maintaining natural and comfortable eye contact is vital because it shows that the subject of the conversation is important.

Lean slightly toward the person. This action expresses interest and involvement. It also forces you to pay attention because you are physically involving yourself in the conversation.

Open posture. Open posture is a way to use your body to show that you are receptive. Otherwise, you might seem like you are introverted or unconcerned. Avoid crossed arms or tense body language.

Relax. Sitting in a relaxed position shows that you are ready to hear what the other person has to say. It also shows that you have cleared your mind, are not preoccupied with other issues, and are capable of giving your undivided attention.

Nonverbal communication is not just FELOR. It also includes cues such as voice volume, voice tone, facial expression, movement, and distance.

	Do's	Don'ts
Eyes	Maintain good eye contact	Blank staring, glaring, wandering eyes, no eye contact
Voice Volume	Speak loudly enough to be heard clearly	Too soft or too loud
Voice Tone	Express interest	Sarcasm, mocking
Facial Expression	Warm, open expression	Yawning, sighing, looking blank
Movement	Lean forward slightly	Leaning away, tapping feet, squirming
Distance	Arm's length	Too close, too far

Nonverbal Communication Activity 1

Goals

1. To reinforce FELOR
2. To demonstrate the basic attending skills
3. To become aware of the specific nonverbal skills involved in communicating effectively
4. To compare the response of the speaker when attending and nonattending skills are used

Directions

Part A

Find a partner (again, someone you don't know very well). Decide who is "A" or "B." Person A tells person B something that they enjoyed doing over the weekend. However, person B suddenly lost all memory and does not remember any of the nonverbal communication skills just learned. Spend no more than a minute discussing the topic. Reverse roles.

Part B

With the same partners, ask person A to tell person B something they would like to change about themselves. This time, however, person B miraculously regained his/her memory of FELOR. Take another minute and discuss the topic using proper attending skills.

Debrief

Observations. I noticed that . . .
1. During part A what physical reactions did you have when your partner would not listen to you?
2. What were you inclined to do during part A?
3. What was the noise level of the room?
4. What happened to the conversation during part A and then during part B?
5. Compare your reactions to both conversations.

Personal meaning. I realized or learned or it was reconfirmed for me that . . .
1. When comparing conversation A with conversation B, what conclusions can you come to?
2. Which skill seems to have made the biggest impression on you?

Action Plan. How can you apply what you realized or learned about yourself in another situation? In the future I will . . .
1. How can this exercise help you become a better listener?
2. What can you ask your friends or family members to do to be better listeners?

Personal Thoughts and Notes

Observations. I noticed that . . .

Personal meaning. I learned or realized or it was reconfirmed for me that . . .

Action plan. How can you apply what you realized or learned about yourself in another situation? In the future I will . . .

Student Leadership Training

ROADBLOCKS

Roadblocks prohibit effective communication. They can cause people to become defensive and to feel unaccepted, rejected, or judged. In addition, roadblocks show lack of respect and distrust. Keep in mind that there may be times when some of these statements are appropriate, **but** . . . the main objective of this section is to raise your awareness of how these roadblocks can hinder effective communication.

Common Communication Roadblocks

Giving Solutions, Advising

For example, "Why don't you . . ." and "If I were you . . ."
- implies the incompetence of the person to solve their own problems; may cause dependency
- hinders people from thoroughly analyzing their problems and taking into account all possible alternatives

Warning, Threatening

For example, "You have to, or . . ." and "If you don't, then . . . "
- can lead to resistance, anger, and resentment
- can cause intimidation

Praising, Agreeing

For example, "Yeah, that sounds good!" or "You're so smart!" and "It sounds like you're right to me."
- can be condescending

- can cause anxiety when expectations fail to match the person's perception of his/herself
- doesn't assist people with evaluating their problems

Persuading, Arguing

For example, "Yes, but . . . ", "You're wrong because . . . "
- provokes defensive and distrustful behavior
- promotes a feeling of inferiority
- can cause the person to shut out suggestions

Name-Calling, Ridiculing

For example, "You big baby." or "What's the matter with you?"
- can cause feelings of defensiveness and inadequacy
- can lower a person's self-image
- can promote a negative reaction through physical or verbal means

Reassuring, Sympathizing

For example, " Don't worry, everything will be fine." Or, "You'll make it through . . ."
- may cause a person to feel discouraged and misunderstood
- may result in the avoidance of resolving an issue

Probing, Questioning

For example, "Who . . . ", "How . . . ", "Why . . ."
- asking too many questions can divert from the person's intent or main concern

Ordering, Commanding

For example, "You need to . . ." or "You must . . ."
- may result in the person feeling compelled to retaliate
- may result in the person feeling inadequate

Moralizing, Preaching

For example, "You ought to . . . " or "It is your responsibility to . . . "
- can cause the person to become defensive
- may cause the person to feel obligated to the speaker

Sarcasm

For example, "Well that's just a great idea."
- can infer a lack of interest in a person's problems
- may cause the person to feel avoided

Analyzing, Diagnosing

For example, "Well, your problem is . . . ", "You're not thinking this through . . . "
- can be wrong and can mislead the person
- can cause the person to feel trapped and not acknowledged

Criticizing, Blaming, Judging, Comparing

For example, "What's wrong with you?" or "How could you do that?" and "Why can't you be more like your sister?
- may cause the person to feel inept and useless
- may cause the person to cut off communication for fear of negative feedback

Roadblocks Activity 1

Goals

1. To practice identifying the common roadblocks to effective communication.
2. To become familiar with the meaning of the roadblocks so you can become more aware of their negative effects.

Directions

In pairs, take turns reading the statements on the following page, while the listener fills in the blank with the appropriate roadblock from the list provided:

Threatening	Warning	Name-calling
Agreeing	Preaching	Arguing
Ordering	Commanding	Diagnosing
Sympathizing	Sarcasm	Diverting
Probing	Judging	Blaming
Moralizing	Analyzing	Withdrawal
Reassuring	Ridiculing	Criticizing
Over-praising	Advising	Giving solutions
Lecturing	Excusing	

After completing the roadblocks worksheet, discuss with your partner the following questions:

- Which roadblocks were particularly difficult to identify?
- Which roadblocks do you use with other people?
- Which roadblock seemed most offensive to you?
- How can you avoid using these roadblocks?
- What situations prompt you to use roadblocks?
- How do you respond when someone blocks your communication?
- How does your partner respond?

Roadblocks Worksheet

1. _____ "That was such a stupid idea."

2. _____ "It doesn't matter if you failed this test; you're smart anyway."

3. _____ "This is so simple. I don't understand why you're having a problem with it."

4. _____ "Well, that's great. Why don't you go try to run the world?"

5. _____ "You should tell her or else it will weigh on your conscience forever."

6. _____ "Your problem is that you rely on your boyfriend too much."

7. _____ "You're such a whiner!"

8. _____ "That's so amazing! I can't believe you thought of that. I wish I could be like you."

9. _____ "Yeah I guess . . . you figure it out."

10. _____ "That's nice. Guess what happened with me. It's so much more exciting!"

Roadblocks Activity 2

Goals

1. To review and reinforce the various roadblocks to effective communication.
2. To be creative and have fun!

Directions

Form yourselves into triads (groups of 3). The teacher will assign a specific roadblock to each group. Using the list of roadblocks in Activity 1, create and perform a skit that will illustrate the communication barrier. After each skit, the rest of the class will identify the appropriate roadblock.

Debrief

Observations. I noticed that . . .
1. As a performer, what was difficult about portraying the roadblock?
2. What did it feel like when you received the roadblock?
3. What seemed evident to you while watching the performances?
4. What were some common reactions to the roadblocks?

Personal meaning. I realized or learned or it was reconfirmed for me that . . . .
1. What roadblocks do you frequently use?
2. How have the performances increased your awareness of using roadblocks?
3. How has the role-playing clarified the individual roadblocks for you?

Action plan. How can you apply what you realized or learned about yourself in another situation? In the future I will . . .
1. What will you do differently as a result of watching these skits?
2. What difficulty do you imagine will prevent you from applying what you learned?
3. What can you do to make your friends and and family members become more aware of how they prevent effective communication?

Personal Thoughts and Notes

Observations. I noticed that . . .

Personal meaning. I learned or realized or it was reconfirmed for me that . . .

Action plan. How can you apply what you realized or learned about yourself in another situation? In the future I will . . .

LISTENING

"Listening opens the door to meaningful communication."
—Diane Taub

Listening is an integral part of everyday life often taken for granted, but it is a valuable skill in becoming a peer leader. If listening skills are well developed, they can be powerful tools for successful communication.

Skilled listeners never passively absorb the words spoken by others. They work to understand, accept, and respond to both the meaning and the feelings of the person speaking.

Techniques of Attentive Listening

1. Have a good attitude. Present a warm and open manner. Act and sound interested in order to encourage the speaker to continue talking.
2. The listener should avoid agreeing or disagreeing and instead use neutral words. To stimulate conversation, you should use gestures such as nodding of the head or using expressions such as, "Can you tell me more . . . ?"
3. Paraphrase and clarify. To avoid misinterpretation, summarizing and restating your understanding of the speaker's position and feelings is important—it shows your attentiveness and gives an opportunity for clarification.

Active vs. Empathic

With effective communication, differentiating between *active* and *empathic* listening is crucial. **Active listening** (listening for content) is being more than a passive observer. It's helpful to use a number of techniques to get as much *content or information* out of the listening experience as possible.

On the other hand, **empathic listening** (listening for feeling) is used to develop a relationship of trust so that the listener can understand how the speaker is feeling.

Guidelines to Successful Empathic Listening

1. Use the FELOR skills that you learned in the Nonverbal Communication unit.
2. Focus on the speaker; listen to *what* the person is saying.
3. Be attentive to the nonverbal cues; pay attention to the speaker's feelings.
4. Listen. The best way to help someone is by giving them your undivided attention.
5. Show that you understand what is being said by paraphrasing and using nonverbal gestures.

Watch out for these common mistakes
- Concentrating on the facts and ignoring feelings
- Neglecting to use important FELOR skills
- Talking more about your personal experiences rather than focusing on the speaker's specific situation
- Using the common roadblocks (e.g., sarcasm, withdrawal, reassuring)

Listening Activity 1

Goals

1. To demonstrate how your tone of voice reflects what you are saying and how you are feeling.
2. To determine the way in which your tone of voice influences how the listener interprets what you are saying and how you are feeling.

Directions

The teacher will divide the class into groups of six to eight people and assign a portion of the following sample statements to each group. Each person in the group will alternate reading the sentences with the appropriate feeling. The rest of the group will listen actively and determine the emotion behind the sentences.

1. Keep it down! I can't concentrate on my homework.
2. I've never seen him so pissed off before.
3. We're going to the Bahamas for summer break!

4. I wish my math teacher would give me a break.
5. Oh wow! This homework is so exciting.
6. You can do it all night long!
7. I can't believe it's already Thursday; prom is only two days away!
8. I wish we didn't have to go to summer school.
9. I'm really worried about her. She's been doing a lot of pot lately.
10. He better stop talkin' $%!+ behind my back!
11. They expect so much of me; I can't take it anymore.
12. My boyfriend keeps pressuring me to have sex with him.
13. Jessica seems really depressed lately; I'm worried about her.
14. I don't think we can trust this guy.
15. Recently, my parents have been fighting a lot.

As you can see, the way you read these sentences can affect their meaning (e.g., you can read a sentence with seriousness or sarcasm). Therefore, attentive listening is very important in distinguishing the emotions expressed through tone of voice.

Debrief

Observations. I noticed that . . .
1. How effectively did the speaker communicate the emotions?
2. What would happen if the questions were read with a tone of voice conveying a different emotion?

Personal meaning. I realized or learned or it was reconfirmed for me that . . .
1. What did you realize when someone misinterpreted the emotion of any one of the statements?
2. What stood out for you as the speaker was reading the sample sentences?
3. How did listening to the various interpretations help you?

Action plan. How can you apply what you realized or learned about yourself in another situation? In the future I will . . .
1. How might you pay more attention to tone of voice in the future?
2. What can you do to help others understand what you are feeling?

Personal Thoughts and Notes

Observations. I noticed that . . .

Personal meaning. I learned or realized or it was reconfirmed for me that . . .

Action plan. How can you apply what you realized or learned about yourself in another situation? In the future I will . . .

Paraphrasing

Paraphrasing is a crucial component of listening. It allows speakers to know that you are listening to them and that you understand what they have just expressed to you.

Paraphrasing also provides a method for clarification if miscommunication or misinterpretation occurs between the speaker and the listener. It promotes further communication by showing interest through attempts to understand the situation as well as the speaker's feelings and attitude.

Listening actively enables the listeners to restate what has just been said in their own words. The speaker in turn can correct or validate the listener's perception of the situation, thereby ensuring that both are on the same page.

Without this clarification it is difficult for the listener to fully comprehend the feelings and attitude of the speaker. It also presents an opportunity for the speakers to express exactly how they feel, enabling them to see the situation more clearly and act accordingly.

Listening Activity 2

Goals

1. To provide an opportunity to practice paraphrasing and to use the active listening skills that you have learned so far
2. To learn more about each other
3. To reinforce the effectiveness of paying attention to the people that you are listening to, as well as understanding the importance of responding appropriately to them

Directions

Break off into pairs. For three to four minutes, one student will talk about a situation while the other listens while using FELOR and active and empathic listening skills. Think about one of the following possible situations:

- A problem you are having with a family member
- A situation at school that is causing you grief
- A problem you are having with a friend (male or female)

At the end of the allotted time, the listener will practice paraphrasing the speaker's situation by completing the following sentence: "The one thing I heard you say that seemed most important to you was . . ."
Repeat the activity, switching roles.

Debrief

Observations. I noticed that . . .
1. What did your partner do to make you feel that he/she was paying attention to you?
2. How did it feel when your partner correctly paraphrased your primary concern?
3. What encouraged you to keep talking?

Personal meaning. I realized or learned or it was reconfirmed for me that . . .
1. What would you say was the most important thing you learned about yourself as a result of this conversation?
2. What enabled you to disclose more information about yourself?
3. In what way was this conversation the same or different for you as compared to other conversations that you may have had?

Action plan. How can you apply what you realized or learned about yourself in another situation? In the future I will . . .
1. What will you do differently as a result of learning the significance of paraphrasing?
2. What difficulty do you imagine you will have in applying any of these listening skills?
3. How might learning these skills benefit you in having a more meaningful conversation with others (family or friends)?

Personal Thoughts and Notes

Observations. I noticed that . . .

Personal meaning. I learned or realized or it was reconfirmed for me that . . .

Action plan. How can you apply what you realized or learned about yourself in another situation? In the future I will . . .

QUESTIONING

Student Leadership Training

QUESTIONING

Learning how to ask effective questions can truly enhance communication. Questioning is a skill that takes practice and considerable effort to master. Effective questioning can help to maintain open lines of communication, just as ineffective questioning can prohibit communication from developing into a more meaningful conversation.

It is also important to be aware of some of the other purposes that effective questioning can serve. Asking good questions signals to other people that we are actively following conversation and are working to understand what they are saying. This sometimes helps people to pause and think more deeply about a situation and their response to it.

The key technique involved in effective questioning is to evaluate the situation and understand what kind of question is appropriate. There are two different approaches to questioning: **closed questions** and **open-ended questions**. Another form of questioning commonly misused is the "why" question. Be aware that asking a "why" question can sometimes put a person on the defensive, causing the speaker to withdraw from the conversation. When questioning skills are performed the right way, people will feel like they are part of a dialogue rather than an interrogation.

Closed Questions

Closed questions are useful if you need to know the facts of a situation. Usually closed questions begin with *who, what, when,* and *where,* and tend to generate "yes" or "no" answers or one-word answers. Because closed questions ask only for factual information, they do not delve into the feelings, attitude, and emotions behind the facts and generally do not allow for follow-up questions. Therefore, we must use a combination of closed questions and open-ended questions to fully understand what the person is saying.

Open-Ended Questions

Open-ended questions are useful in allowing speakers to explore their feelings. They typically begin with *how,* or words or phrases that encourage speakers to tell you more about the situation or their areas of concern.

Example Questions

Closed:

"Do you like school?"

Open-ended:

"What is it about English that makes it your favorite subject?"

Closed:

"Is this the way you want our relationship to be?"

Open-ended:

"What kind of relationship are you looking for?"

Closed:

"Are you angry?"

Open-ended:

"What do your parents do that makes you so angry?"

Closed:

"Are you coming to the party tonight?"

Open-ended:

"What do you think might happen at the party?"

As you can see, closed questions ask for **factual information** whereas open-ended questions **encourage you to elaborate more on the details of your situation, as well as your feelings.** However, it is important to note that a good conversation requires a good combination of both closed questions and open-ended questions.

Questioning Activity 1

Goals

1. To introduce questioning as a skill
2. To practice changing a closed question to an open-ended question
3. To hear the different response of a closed versus an open-ended question
4. To be aware of the effects of a "why" question

Directions

On your own, change each of the following closed questions to an open-ended question. Once you have completed all the questions, find a partner and ask him/her the closed question first, then the open-ended question you have just created.

1. How often do you fight with your best friend?

2. Are you excited to go to college?

3. Is everything going well with your boyfriend?

4. Are you looking forward to your family vacation?

5. How do you like my haircut?

6. Are you going to talk to Kelly at the party?

7. Do you enjoy reading our English book?

8. Why don't you get along with your parents?

9. Do people accept your sexual orientation?

10. Are you sad?

Debrief

Observations. I noticed that . . .
1. How difficult was it to change the closed questions to open-ended questions?
2. How did your partner's responses vary when asked open-ended and closed questions?

Personal meaning. I realized or learned or it was reconfirmed for me that . . .
1. How would being able to create an open-ended question be helpful?
2. What is the most important aspect of this skill in helping to open the lines of communication?

3. By asking effective questions, how are you more able to help the person you are talking to?

Action plan. How can you apply what you realized or learned about yourself in another situation? In the future I will . . .
   1. In what other situations can learning to ask open-ended questions be helpful?
   2. When might you find yourself in a situation where changing a closed question to an open-ended question be helpful?
   3. When might you want to ask a closed question?

Personal Thoughts and Notes

Observations. I noticed that . . .

Personal meaning. I learned or realized or it was reconfirmed for me that . . .

Action plan. How can you apply what you realized or learned about yourself in another situation? In the future I will . . .

Questioning Activity 2

Goals

1. To practice asking both open-ended and closed questions
2. To recognize the benefits of using both methods of questioning, depending on the particular situation
3. To learn when to ask the appropriate kind of question to enhance communication
4. To be able to distinguish between and give examples of open-ended and closed questions

Directions

The teacher will ask for two volunteers from the entire class. Each volunteer must be prepared to tell about something that has happened recently. The volunteers will leave the room, while the teacher instructs the rest of the class to ask **only** "closed questions" to the first volunteer and **only** "open-ended" questions to the second volunteer for approximately five minutes each. After the allotted time, use a combination of open-ended and closed questions to gather any remaining details for either story.

Debrief

Observations. I noticed that . . .
1. How were the responses different for each volunteer?
2. How do you suppose the volunteer felt while the class was asking only closed questions? (As the volunteer, how did you feel?)
3. What were some of the reactions to the "why" questions?
4. How was it helpful to be able to ask a combination of questions?

Personal meaning. I realized or learned or it was reconfirmed for me that . . .
1. What stood out for you while listening to each kind of question?
2. What difficulties did you encounter while having to ask the volunteers questions?
3. What else could happen if you are asked **only** closed or "why" questions?

Action plan. How can you apply what you realized or learned about yourself in another situation? In the future I will . . .
1. What will you do differently next time you are speaking to a stranger?

2. What difficulty do you imagine will prevent you from asking appropriate questions?
3. How will learning to ask effective questions help you in your role as student leader?

Personal Thoughts and Notes

Observations. I noticed that . . .

Personal meaning. I learned or realized or it was reconfirmed for me that . . .

Action plan. How can you apply what you realized or learned about yourself in another situation? In the future I will . . .

Student Leadership Training

"I" MESSAGES

"I" messages are important in effective communication because they let the speaker know that the listener is giving his/her own feelings about the issue at hand. They show the listener's concern in a non-threatening way. We tend to use "You" messages because we are more comfortable generalizing and not personalizing our experiences for fear of being judged. We feel more vulnerable when we talk about ourselves, yet "I" messages are one of the most important ways in which we can relay personal sentiment effectively.

"I" messages	"You" messages
Describe why you are affected by what is said	Blame, judge, convey disapproval
Allow you to state your opinion without offending the other person	Are disrespectful
Let you express your feelings	Isolate you from the situation

A typical I-message consists of three parts:*
> "I feel [state feeling] when you [describe specific behavior] because [state how it affects you]."

*The behavior can be stated either before or after the feeling.

Examples:
1. "I feel **sad** when you **make fun of me** because **it hurts my feelings**."
   Not: "You always make fun of me. I don't want to be friends with you."
2. "When you **flake out on me at the last minute** it really **annoys** me because **I rearranged my schedule to do something with you**."
   Not: "You're so unreliable. I never want to make plans with you again."

"I" Messages Activity 1

Goals

1. To introduce the concept of an "I" message vs. a "You" message
2. To learn how to construct a three-part "I" message
3. To differentiate between both types of messages
4. To understand how each type of message impacts the listener

Directions

Using the following situations, construct both a "You" message and an "I" message and write it in the space provided. Then find a partner and read your responses to each other.

Situations

1. After working really hard on a research project and being reassured by your teacher that you were doing fine, your teacher gives you an F on the project.

   "You" message:

   "I" message:

2. Your best friend constantly criticizes and nags you about your faults.

   "You" message:

   "I" message:

3. On a day that you were home sick from school, a classmate volunteered you to complete an assignment that he knew you would not feel comfortable doing.

   "You" message:

   "I" message:

4. When you disagree with your parents, they embarrass you in front of your friends.

    "You" message:

    "I" message:

5. Your boyfriend/girlfriend is forty minutes late for a movie date.

    "You" message:

    "I" message:

6. You are in a movie theater and the people behind you constantly comment during the movie.

    "You" message:

    "I" message:

7. Whenever you are on the phone, your mother tries to eavesdrop.

    "You" message:

    "I" message:

8. Your sibling always borrows your clothes without asking for permission.

    "You" message:

    "I" message:

9. Your friend owes you money and has been promising to pay you back for the past three months.

   "You" message:

   "I" message:

10. During your basketball game you get hit and get a bloody nose, but instead of helping you your best friend laughs at you.

    "You" message:

    "I" message:

Debrief

Observations. I noticed that . . .
   1. What difficulties did you encounter while trying to construct the "I" message?
   2. Which type of message seemed to come more naturally to you?
   3. When your partner read the "You" messages to you, how did you react?
   4. When the "I" messages were read, how did you react differently?

Personal meaning. I realized or learned or it was reconfirmed for me that . . .
   1. How can using "I" messages help you develop better relationships with your peers?
   2. What will it take to feel more comfortable in constructing and using "I" message more often?
   3. How does the "You" message prevent effective and open communication?

Action plan. How can you apply what you realized or learned about yourself in another situation? In the future I will . . .
   1. How can you encourage your friends and family members to use "I" messages more often?
   2. What can you do to make the process of using "I" messages more a part of your everyday communication?
   3. What will you do to avoid using "You" messages?

Personal Thoughts and Notes

Observations. I noticed that . . .

Personal meaning. I learned or realized or it was reconfirmed for me that . . .

Action plan. How can you apply what you realized or learned about yourself in another situation? In the future I will . . .

FEEDBACK

Student Leadership Training

FEEDBACK

Working definition of *feedback:*

Telling another person how his or her words and/or actions affect you; in other words, letting another person know how he or she "comes across" to you. Feedback is an honest reaction to how a person affects you. When given properly, it offers people an opportunity to understand themselves better and to change, if they decide to do so.

Feedback helps a person realize what his words and actions "mean" to other people.

In order to give effective feedback, one must construct an "I message" (as learned in the previous section), which will enable one to understand the **facilitative feedback model**. Just like the "I message," the facilitative feedback model has three parts:*

- Be specific about the person's behavior. (Be descriptive and give an example if you can.)
- Tell how the person's behavior makes you feel.
- Tell how his or her behavior affects you.

*Remember: The behavior can be stated either before or after you tell the person how their action or words makes you feel.

Guidelines to Giving Successful Feedback

- Talk about behavior you can see.
- Make it specific.
- Make sure it's relevant.
- It does not necessarily have to be given on the spot—but as soon as possible.
- It should be given directly, not hinted at or filtered through a third party.
- Give the other person a chance to explain.
- Give it caringly.
- Feedback is not feedback when it's meant to hurt—then it's just an attack.

53

- Don't nag or hound people about their behavior unless they have told you that they want your help.
- Avoid being judgmental. (Watch for "right" and "wrong.")
- The way we feel as a result of another's behavior is authentic and genuine. Tell how you feel.
- Avoid sarcasm or a condescending manner when giving feedback.
- Share the positive too.
- Do not give advice—just reactions.

Guidelines to Receiving Feedback

- Ask for it.
- Receive it openly.
- Do not make excuses.
- Acknowledge its value.
- Express appreciation that someone cared enough to give you feedback.
- Discuss it. Don't just say "thank you" and let it drop.
- Indicate what you intend to do with it.
- Watch out for becoming defensive.
- Try to avoid getting mad, seeking revenge, ignoring what's said or the person saying it.
- Don't look for motives or hidden meanings.
- Seek clarification.
- Think about it and try to build on it.
- View feedback as a continuing exploration.

Feedback Activity 1

Goals

1. To introduce the concept of **feedback**
2. To define "feedback" and practice the facilitative feedback model

Directions

Individually, complete the worksheet. Once completed, find a partner and discuss examples with each other.

Practice Using the Facilitative Feedback Model

Remember that there are three parts to the model:

1. Be specific about the person's behavior. (Be descriptive and give an example if you can.)
2. Tell how the person's behavior makes you feel.
3. Tell how his/her behavior affects you.

Think of something that your parent did or said to you recently that made you feel special. Give this parent effective feedback using the facilitative feedback model by writing an "I" message in the space provided.

_____
_____
_____
_____
_____

Think of something that your parent did or said to you recently that made you very angry. Give this parent effective feedback using the facilitative feedback model by writing an "I" message in the space provided.

_____
_____
_____
_____
_____

Think of something that your friend did or said to you recently that gave you a pleasant feeling. Give this friend effective feedback using the facilitative feedback model by writing an "I" message in the space provided.

_____
_____
_____
_____
_____

Think of something that your friend did or said to you recently that gave you an unpleasant feeling. Give this friend effective feedback using the facilitative feedback model by writing an "I" message in the space provided.

_____
_____
_____
_____
_____

Think of someone else who did or said something to you recently that gave you a pleasant feeling. Give this person effective feedback using the facilitative feedback model by writing an "I" message in the space provided.

_____
_____
_____
_____
_____

Think of someone else who did or said something to you recently that gave you an unpleasant feeling. Give this friend effective feedback using the facilitative feedback model by writing an "I" message in the space provided.

_____
_____
_____
_____
_____

Once you've completed the worksheet, meet with your partner to discuss the following:

- Check each of your statements. Does each one contain the three parts of the model? Were you at any time judgmental, critical, or offering advice? Were you honest about your feelings? Make any corrections you think could improve the quality of these feedback statements.

- What was the most difficult part of using the facilitative feedback model?

Feedback Activity 2

Goals

1. To practice giving effective feedback verbally
2. To recognize the effective methods of giving and receiving feedback
3. To become more aware of the feelings associated with giving and receiving feedback

Directions

In groups of five form a circle and place an empty chair in the center. Think of a person to whom you would like to give feedback. Then, one at a time, give the group background information about the scenario without revealing any names. Now imagine that person sitting in the chair and give him/her feedback using an "I message" with all three parts.

Debrief

Observations. I noticed that . . .
1. What difficulties did you have verbalizing the feedback you gave to the "imaginary" person?
2. How do you suppose your "imaginary" person would have reacted to your feedback?
3. As an observer in the group, how comfortable did each person seem giving feedback?
4. If you had been in the empty chair, how would you have felt receiving the feedback?

Personal meaning. I realized or learned or it was confirmed for me that . . .
1. How can the facilitative feedback model help you express your unpleasant feelings?
2. How can the facilitative feedback model help you express your pleasant feelings?
3. How does using the facilitative feedback model make you more aware of your feelings?

Action plan. How can you apply what you've learned or realized about yourself to another situation? In the future I will . . .
1. What will you do differently when someone affects your feelings?
2. What will prevent you from using the facilitative feedback model?
3. Who will benefit the most from your learning this skill?

Personal Thoughts and Notes

Observations. I noticed that . . .

Personal meaning. I learned or realized or it was reconfirmed for me that . . .

Action plan. How can you apply what you realized or learned about yourself in another situation? In the future I will . . .

REVIEW OF SKILLS

Student Leadership Training

REVIEW OF SKILLS

Review Activity 1

Goals

1. To review and practice all the communication skills learned thus far
2. To be able to identify specific skills while observing another person's conversation

Directions

Create groups of three (triads). For about three to four minutes, discuss any one of the following topics:

- A situation concerning a family member
- A problem you are having with your friend
- A school related issue
- Anything else that is on your mind that you would like to discuss

Take turns being the observer, the listener, and the speaker. Remember, each time you switch roles, take about three to four minutes.
As the observer, make sure you take notes on the observation sheet.

Observation Sheet

During the discussion between the speaker and the listener, *the observer* should note:
- What active listening techniques did the listener use?
- What did the listener do that was effective?
- What could the listener have done differently?

When time is called . . .

Ask the speaker:
- What did the listener do that encouraged you to talk more?
- Did the listener do anything that discouraged you from talking?
- How did you feel at the end of this discussion?
- What did the listener do that you found especially helpful?

Ask the listener:
- What made it difficult or easy for you to listen?
- Which techniques were easiest for you to use? Which were the most difficult?
- What active listening techniques would you like to practice more?

Debrief

Observations. I noticed that . . .
1. Which role was most comfortable for you? What made it so comfortable?
2. How was the feedback from the observer helpful?
3. What did you notice while you were asking each other the various questions (as the speaker and listener)?
4. How difficult was it to identify the various skills?

Personal meaning. I learned or realized or it was reconfirmed for me that . . .
1. What impact do you feel learning these skills will have on you?
2. Who will benefit the most by your knowledge of these skills?
3. What will you need to do in order to become completely comfortable using these skills?
4. How has your awareness of these skills increased over time?

Action plan. How can you apply what you realized or learned about yourself in another situation? In the future I will . . .
1. In what situations can you imagine yourself applying these skills?
2. As a result of learning these skills, what will greatly be improved?

Personal Thoughts and Notes

Observations. I noticed that . . .

Personal meaning. I learned or realized or it was reconfirmed for me that . . .

Action plan. How can you apply what you realized or learned about yourself in another situation? In the future I will . . .

VALUES

Values Underlying Student Leadership

Human interaction, behavior, and personal beliefs are based on an underlying set of values. Our student leadership training and program are based on the following basic guidelines:

1. Individuals have the right and responsibility to maintain and defend their own convictions in the face of adversity. **If this is not upheld, individuals may undermine their own self-worth.**
2. Individuals have the responsibility to respect the values of others and be tolerant of their differences. **Awareness of these differences not only opens eyes to diversity but also allows for personal growth through open-mindedness. Our personal decisions and daily interactions should reflect this respect for both others and ourselves.**
3. Peer relationships, self-awareness, and personal growth are most successfully achieved through open and effective communication. **Willingness to share personal experiences and the ability to listen attentively is the foundation of our student leadership program.**

Values Activity 1

Goals

1. To become aware of the source of our values
2. To understand the perspective of each others values

Directions

Write down something that you are prejudiced against. This process should be done anonymously so that people will write freely and honestly. Then the teacher will gather everything that was written and will write the results on the board for everyone to see. Discuss with the class the values behind each prejudice and the possible reasons people may become prejudiced. (For example: obesity. People who value health, physical fitness, and self image might believe that obese people are lazy and have no concern for their body image.)

Debrief

Observations. I noticed that . . .
1. What did you observe while the various issues were being discussed?
2. What was most surprising to you about the results?
3. How did you react to your peers prejudices?

Personal meaning. I realized or learned or it was reconfirmed for me that . . .
1. How comfortable was it to discuss with the class your specific prejudices?
2. Where do the majority of your values come from?

Action plan. How can you apply what you realized or learned about yourself in another situation? In the future I will . . .
1. How will this affect your discussions in training?
2. How will this affect your ability to relate to your peers in future interactions?

Personal Thoughts and Notes

Observations. I noticed that . . .

Personal meaning. I learned or realized or it was reconfirmed for me that . . .

Action plan. How can you apply what you realized or learned about yourself in another situation? In the future I will . . .

Values Activity 2

Goals

1. To identify personal values
2. To become more aware of what is important to your fellow peers

Directions

Part A

The following is a list of concepts that most people value. Cut a piece of paper into six small pieces. Choose the three most important values and write them down on three pieces of paper. Then, choose the three values that are least important to you and that you would be most willing to "throw away" and write them down on the remaining three pieces of paper. Then, put those three pieces in the center of the room and your teacher will read off the values that were "thrown away."

Financial Security
Honesty
Popularity
Self-respect
Physical/Mental Health
Friendships

Power/Authority
Religion
Justice/Equality
Faith
Intelligence
Family Relationships

Directions

Part B

Think about a person who knows you really well. What would he or she say are the three most important values and the three least important values for you?

Most important values:

1. _____

2. _____

3. _____

Least important values:

4. _____

5. _____

6. _____

Directions

Part C

Then reverse it. What do you think are the three values that the person you thought about in part B values most for him- or herself? Indicate your answers with a 1, 2, and 3. Then choose the three values that are least important to that person that he/she would be most willing to throw away. These values are 4, 5, and 6.

_____ Financial Security   _____ Power/Authority

_____ Honesty   _____ Religion

_____ Popularity   _____ Justice/Equality

_____ Self-respect   _____ Faith

_____ Physical/Mental Health   _____ Intelligence

_____ Friendships   _____ Family Relationships

Now, give this worksheet back to that person and discuss the differences between the values that you chose for yourself, the values that you think the person in part B chose for you, and the values that you chose for the person in part B.

Debrief (Parts A, B, and C)

Observations. I noticed that . . .

1. What were some of the difficulties when trying to determine your most important values?
2. What were some of the difficulties when "throwing away" your least important values?
3. How close did this person come to choosing the values that were most and least important to you?
4. What surprised you about this person's responses?

Personal meaning. I realized or learned or it was reconfirmed for me that . . .

1. How easy or difficult was it to determine which values were the most and least important to you?
2. What did you realize about yourself when comparing your answers with the person who knows you really well?
3. How does your perception of yourself compare to the way others see you?

Action plan. How can you apply what you realized or learned about yourself in another situation? In the future I will . . .

1. Knowing what values are most and least important to you, how will this affect your decision-making process in the future?
2. By understanding how others perceive you, how will this affect your training groups?

Personal Thoughts and Notes

Observations. I noticed that . . .

Personal meaning. I learned or realized or it was reconfirmed for me that . . .

Action plan. How can you apply what you realized or learned about yourself in another situation? In the future I will . . .

Values Activity 3

Goals

1. To gain a better sense of how your peers view certain characteristics of debatable situations
2. To become more aware of the importance of respecting another person's views, especially when they are different than your own

Directions

Form into groups of five or six people, and try as best as you can to reach a consensus ranking the people in descending order of preference (worst first) and decide why you chose that order.

1. Ken is a homophobic baseball team captain who ensures that homosexuals are not placed on the teams.
2. Tom is physically and verbally abusing his girlfriend, Meg.
3. Susie is selling drugs to the middle school students.
4. Joe is friends with David, the unpopular student at school, just because David's father has floor seats to the local basketball team. David constantly gives gifts to Joe in order to maintain their friendship, but when Joe is around his other friends he is the first one to insult David and start rumors about him.
5. Dan is bringing a gun to school for "protection." He is being bullied so he takes the weapon with him "just in case."
6. Jill, age 16, is getting an abortion because she does not want to keep the baby even though her boyfriend is undecided.

Debrief

Observations. I noticed that . . .
1. What did you observe while you were discussing the various characters?
2. What happened when people disagreed with the order?
3. What was the most difficult part in coming to consensus?

Personal meaning. I realized or learned or it was reconfirmed for me that . . .
1. How has this discussion affected your convictions toward your values?

2. It is important to be tolerant and respectful of how your peers view a variety of values. How has this activity been helpful in understanding this statement?

Action plan. How can you apply what you realized or learned about yourself in another situation? In the future I will . . .
   1. How might what you have just realized or learned about yourself be helpful in training or with your relationships with your friends or family?
   2. When facing controversy in the future, how will you be better prepared?

Personal Thoughts and Notes

Observations. I noticed that . . .

Personal meaning. I learned or realized or it was reconfirmed for me that . . .

Action plan. How can you apply what you realized or learned about yourself in another situation? In the future I will . . .

Values Activity 4

Goals

1. To understand how your behavior is affected by values
2. To more deeply examine the values that are important to you

Directions

Part A

Think of any three values that are important to you. For each value, write down an example of a specific experience that demonstrates your belief in that value. (For example: I value physical health so I go to the gym three times a week.)

Value: _____

Demonstration of Belief:

_____
_____
_____
_____

Value: _____

Demonstration of Belief:

_____
_____
_____
_____

Value: _____

Demonstration of Belief:

_____
_____
_____
_____

Directions

Part B

Find a partner and discuss with each other the three values that you've each chosen. Then discuss the following:

- How difficult was it for you to come up with your values?
- How difficult was it for you to give an example of the values in which you believe?
- Were there any actions not consistent with your values? Please explain.
- Who has had the greatest influence on you in determining what you value? And how have they influenced you?

DECISION MAKING

Student Leadership Training

DECISION MAKING

We are always making decisions. From the time we get up in the morning until we go to bed at night, we are faced with decisions. Life is a continuous decision-making process.

No matter what we do, we have to live with it. Unfortunately, many people tend to live their lives haphazardly and spend little time approaching life in a thoughtful way.

We all want to make decisions that will improve our lifestyle. We will present a five-step decision-making process that can serve as a plan of action to assist you in gaining more control over your life and enhance your lifestyle. Also, knowing this method could assist you by providing you with a plan of action when helping others with a problem or a decision. But remember, they are responsible for solving their own problems.

Five-Step Decision-Making Process

1. Identify the central issue or problem.

2. Explore the issue or problem.

3. Choose a next step.

4. Act on your choice.

5. Evaluate the results.

Step 1: Identify the Central Issue or Problem

Pinpointing all the aspects of the problem or situation is very important. It might be helpful to answer these kinds of questions:

- What is the problem?
- When does it occur and under what circumstances?
- Who else is involved or who else contributes to the problem?
- Who or what interferes with making a decision?
-

Sometimes the pressure of deciding can be so overwhelming that it prevents us from taking any action at all. If we first sort out and clearly identify the issue or the problem, then the other steps of the decision-making process make more sense.

Step 2: Explore the Issue or Problem

Every situation involves a weighing and balancing of the many forces that are part of the problem. As we attempt to explore a situation, it is necessary to look at the alternatives and the consequences of any decision. To *not* make a decision, of course, is to make a decision. The alternatives and consequences of being indecisive can also be examined. It is important to be as clear as possible regarding our values and attitudes in relation to alternatives and consequences.

Step 3: Choose a Next Step

After considering the alternatives and consequences to various problems, and weighing the pros and cons of the situation, you can now make a decision. It is important to remember that others can be helpful in exploring the alternatives with you. However, the final decision should be your own.

Step 4: Act on Your Choice

Once you have made a decision and decided on a next step, it is time to put that choice into action. Acting on your decisions can sometimes make you anxious. You now realize that your decision has been made and that you must face the situation and take full responsibility for the decision.

Step 5: Evaluate the Results

The final step involves analyzing the outcomes of what you have done. You now need to ask the question: How are you feeling about what has happened as a result of your decision? Your personal value system will be of help in evaluating the results. You may begin the process of making decisions again. Based on results from other decisions, new alternatives may be chosen and new directions sought. You also may realize that the outcome of your decision has affected you positively, causing you to feel very proud.

Decision-Making Activity 1

Goals

1. To explore the process of decision making
2. To become more aware that all decisions have consequences

Directions

Divide a piece of paper in half. Mark the top half of the page "Good Decisions" and mark the bottom half of the page "Poor Decisions." Thinking back over some important decisions you have made over the past six months, categorize them according to results. Write key words describing the decision in the appropriate section. Once you have completed this exercise, find three other group members. Look at the "Good Decisions" section and ask each other the following questions:

- How did I come to make these decisions?
- Who was influential in my making the decision?
- How many of these decisions were a result of my having received help from others?

Ask these same questions as you look at the section titled "Poor Decisions."

Decision-Making Activity 2

Goals

1. To introduce the students to the process of responsible decision making
2. To present a five-step decision-making process
3. To explore/practice the process of decision making

Directions

With a partner, practice working through a problem and making decisions using the following worksheet. Below are some suggested problems:

- What should you do after high school graduation?
- You have just seen someone cheating on an exam. Should you tell anyone?
- All your friends have become sexually active. You feel the pressure but you are unsure of your readiness to have sex. Should you have sex or not?
- Your parents have refused to let you go to a concert that you have been planning to go to for a long time. What should you do?
- Any other problem that is on your mind.

Problem-Solving Worksheet

1. Identify your problem. Be as specific as possible.
2. Explore the issue or problem. List as many alternatives as you can think of and weigh the pros (positives) and cons (negatives).

Alternative 1: _____

Pros	Cons

Alternative 2: _____

Pros	Cons

Alternative 3: _____

Pros	Cons

Alternative 4: _____

Pros	Cons

3. Choose a next step (pick the best alternative).

4. Act on your choice.

5. Evaluate the results (this can only be imagined at this point).

Debrief

Observations. I noticed that . . .
1. How was working with a partner beneficial in solving your problem?
2. What was difficult about using the decision-making process?
3. How did you react to your partners suggested alternatives?
4. How did exploring the alternatives with your partner help make your decision easier?

Personal meaning. I realized or learned or it was reconfirmed for me that . . .
1. What seemed to be most helpful to you from this process?
2. What decisions have you made in the past that might have been different had you used the five-step decision-making process?

Action plan. How can you apply what you have realized or learned about yourself in another situation? In the future I will . . .
1. How do you think this five-step process will help you help others?
2. In your personal life, how do you envision using this five-step process?

Personal Thoughts and Notes

Observations. I noticed that . . .

Personal meaning. I learned or realized or it was reconfirmed for me that . . .

Action plan. How can you apply what you realized or learned about yourself in another situation? In the future I will . . .

Student Leadership Training

TEEN ISSUES

Useful Resources for Teen Issues

Another important component of our student leadership program is to be knowledgeable of the various teen issues that we must deal with, either for ourselves or for our peers. We have therefore compiled a useful list of facts and statistics of some of the more serious teen topics. We hope these resources will serve as a brief overview and reference guide for the various issues confronting today's teens. More detailed information can be found by calling some of the listed hotlines and visiting the Web sites referenced in this section. We gathered these resources as a result of contacting "Teen Line" of California. But as you will see, many are national toll-free numbers. We encourage your team members to locate local, state, provincial, or national resources that can be accessed by toll-free telephone or the Internet.

Sexually Transmitted Infections (STIs)

Anyone who is sexually active is susceptible to contract an STI (formerly known as STD), also called venereal diseases. The main way to get an STI is through sexual intercourse or any other sexual contact with someone who already has it. Some basic facts about STIs:
- Most STIs are treatable, but there is no vaccine to prevent them.
- It is possible to have an STI without feeling sick or notice any changes in your body.
- The longer an STI goes untreated, the more damage it can do to your body. If not treated, STIs can cause blindness, sores that will not heal, heart disease, paralysis, deafness, damage to an unborn baby, sterility (the inability to have children), and even death.
- You cannot contract STIs from toilet seats, door knobs, or casual contacts.
- Testing for any STI is confidential and your parents do not have to know.
- Some common STIs include:
    - HIV/AIDS virus

        AIDS is caused by a virus called HIV, which can get into a person's bloodstream and attack the body's immune system. It can be transmitted through the exchange of fluids during vaginal or anal inter-course and during oral sex with an infected person. AIDS can also be spread through blood-to-blood contact by sharing needles or syringes with drug users, or by transfusions of infected blood. It is possible to pass on the virus before or during birth and through breastfeeding. Therefore, babies of women with HIV/AIDS may be born with the infection.

- Herpes
  Herpes can be controlled but is not curable.
- Syphilis
- Gonorrhea
- Venereal warts
- Chlamydia

National AIDS Hotline:	800-342-2437
National AIDS Hotline (Spanish):	800-344-7432
TDY: AIDS Hotline	800-243-7889
National Herpes Hotline	919-361-8488
National STD Hotline	800-227-8922

Drugs/Alcohol

When used in large amounts, over a long period of time, or in the wrong combination, alcohol or drugs can kill. Effects depend on the user's body size and personality. Drugs are **very** unpredictable and their effects on the body differ from person to person. Some of the dangers of experimenting with drugs and/or alcohol are:

- Overdose
- Physical illness
- Accidents
- Use of impure or unknown drugs
- Addiction
- Problem with family, work, school
- AIDS (if needles are shared)
- Death

Alcohol is a liquid drug. It is the most abused drug in the United States in all age groups. Alcohol is a depressant that slows a person's heart rate and breathing and affects the part of the brain that controls mood and emotion.

- Games such as chugging (drinking large amounts of alcohol in a short time) can lead to serious consequences, such as death.
- Mixing alcohol with downers or other drugs is extremely dangerous. Wrong combinations can kill you.
- Drinking or using **any** drugs during pregnancy is extremely dangerous to the unborn baby.
- Drinking and driving can kill you and/or others.

National Drug/Alcohol Info	800-622-2255
American Lung Association	800-LUNG-USA
Heroin Hotline	800-943-7646
Cocaine Hotline	800-262-2463
Marijuana Anonymous	800-766-6020
Nicotine Anonymous	800-642-0666
Alcoholics Anonymous	323-669-2463
Alcoholics Anonymous (Spanish)	323-735-2089
Relapse Prevention Hotline	800-735-2773
Alanon Family Group	877-769-7167

www.drughelp.org
www.drugfreeamerica.org
www.acde.org
www.alcoholics-anonymous.org/ef9docl.html

Suicide

If someone talks to you about suicide, take it seriously. A friend may tell you he or she is thinking of killing him or herself and ask you to keep it a secret. *This is a secret you cannot keep.* To be a good friend, encourage the person talking about suicide to talk to an adult he or she trusts or suggest they call one of the provided numbers to talk to someone about it. If you think someone might be suicidal, don't be afraid to ask. Mentioning suicide will not give the person the idea or push them over the edge. Talking about it **can** prevent it from happening. This crisis period usually lasts only a short time. **With a professional, a suicidal person can get better.**

Important warning signs to watch for:
- Talking about committing suicide
- Preoccupation with death
  - Having a specific plan for committing suicide
  - Dramatic changes in behavior
  - Giving away prized possessions
  - Recent loss of a loved one

Crisis Info Hotline   800-339-6993

www.suicidology.org
www.yellowribbon.org

Child Abuse

Child abuse includes neglect and emotional abuse as well as physical and sexual abuse. One-third of the victims of child abuse are teens. Some studies have shown that one in every three girls and one in every six boys become victims of sexual abuse by the age of eighteen. Usually, the abuser is someone the child knows such as a family member or an adult who is familiar and trusted.

Emotional abuse occurs when the adult(s) in charge frequently or even constantly use screaming, threatening, blaming, sarcasm, and putting down as ways to control. An adult who is always depressed, negative, or picking fights with the other members of the household can also be a source of emotional abuse.

Neglect occurs when parents become detached from their children. *Emotional neglect* may happen because the parents are using drugs or alcohol, or because they have their own problems. It can have serious effects on children and teens. *Physical neglect* occurs when a parent or guardian fails to provide a child or teen with adequate food, shelter, clothing, protection, supervision, and/or medical care.

The following are some signs of physical and sexual abuse:
- Burns, cuts, or bruises
- Injury to the genitals or anus
- Frequent nightmares
- Unexplained fear of certain people or places
- Loss of appetite
- Unexplained mood changes
- Use of drugs or alcohol as a means of escape

If you or someone you know is being abused, it is important to seek help. It is not your fault. Talk to an authority figure rather than keeping abuse a secret. Not telling anyone about abuse can lead to serious consequences.

Child Abuse Hotline   800-540-4000
Child Help USA   800-422-4453

www.abuse-safehaven.org
www.childhelpusa.org

Eating Disorders

Abnormal eating behavior caused by trying to feel better about yourself, to avoid feelings, or to feel like you're in control is not healthy. These types of behaviors are eating disorders. Eating disorders include anorexia nervosa, bulimia, and compulsive overeating. Eating disorders not only cause physical problems, but they are also signs of serious emotional problems. These underlying emotional problems can be significantly more dangerous than obvious life-threatening physical problems because they are harder to diagnose and treat.

Bulimia
This is characterized by binge-eating followed by purging. The purging is generally manifested by throwing up, taking laxatives, or exercising excessively. Bulimics generally have a preoccupation with body image or shape. They will also try to hide the bingeing or purging. Common signs of bulimia include excessive weight loss, scarring on the back of the hand if vomiting is utilized, significant fluctuations in body weight, prolonged severe sore throats, and rotting of teeth.

Anorexia Nervosa
More commonly referred to only as "anorexia," this condition is characterized by starvation, excessive dieting, overexercising, and an unrealistic perception of one's self. Signs of anorexia include loss of more than 15 percent of one's body weight, a gaunt appearance, a refusal to eat, and loss of menstrual periods.

Compulsive Overeating
People who develop this condition cannot control their consumption of food. They may not be overweight and their weights may fluctuate between normal and moderately overweight, to severe obesity.

The Rader Institute Corporate Office   800-841-1515
EDAP (Eating Disorders and Prevention Inc)
    National Referral Service   800-931-2237

www.raderpro.com
www.dietingrecovery.com
www.something-fishy.org

Homosexuality

As an adolescent, it is normal to have questions regarding one's sexual orientation. However, teens often face prejudice. It is important for questioning teens to find a reliable support network if they are having trouble coping with their sexuality. As a peer leader, it is your responsibility to guide these teens to a place where they can feel more comfortable.

Because it is often harder for them to feel accepted into society, gay and lesbian teens are more likely to experience emotional problems. Homosexual teens are at a higher risk for destructive behavior including suicide and substance abuse. Therefore, the following referrals can be useful when dealing with a teen with these problems.

Gay and Lesbian National Hotline   888-843-4564
Gay and Lesbian Youth Talkline   800-773-5540
Lyric Helpline   800-969-6884

www.youth.org
www.glnh.org

Rape and Sexual Abuse

Rape is classified as a forced sexual act and can have very serious repercussions both physically and mentally. Victims need to see a doctor immediately for safety reasons including screening for STIs. As a peer leader, it must be stressed that rape is never someone's fault. Otherwise, the victim might internalize their feelings.

Sexual abuse is repeated sexual violations. It is often inflicted by people the victim knows, such as a family member, friend, or peer. It is important to talk to someone trusted when experiencing this form of abuse.

Rape, Abuse, and Incest National Network Hotline (RAINN)   800-656-4673
Victims of Crime Resource Center   800-842-8467
Asian Rape Crisis Hotline   800-339-3940

www.RAINN.org
www.projectsister.org

Pregnancy

If you or someone you know thinks she might be pregnant, it is very important to get tested at a medical center right away. This can be done confidentially and many times at no charge. If this is an unplanned pregnancy it is important to think through the many options, including keeping the baby, adoption, or abortion.

Planned Parenthood   800-230-7526
Teen Reproductive Health Helpline   888-396-line

www.plannedparenthood.org
www.birthright.org
www.CFOC.org

Birth Control

Birth control serves a necessary function for sexually active teens. It is important to practice safe sex to prevent unwanted pregnancies and various STIs. The following are different methods of birth control.

Abstinence
Abstinence from sexual intercourse is the most effective method of preventing pregnancies and STI/HIV.

Condom
When used properly, condoms are more than 90 percent effective at preventing pregnancy and stopping most STIs. When used with spermicide, condoms are even more effective.

Birth Control Pills

When taken regularly, birth control pills can be up to 99 percent effective in preventing pregnancy. However, birth control pills have no effect on transmission of STIs. They can be obtained from your doctor with a prescription or at a free clinic.

Morning After Pill

This does not stop pregnancy if the egg has already been fertilized. It can only be taken within seventy-two hours after intercourse has taken place. One can access the morning after pill with a prescription from a doctor or it can be obtained for free at Planned Parenthood.

Emergency Contraception Hotline	800-584-9911
Family Planning Referral Hotline	800-942-1054
Planned Parenthood	800-230-7526

www.plannedparenthood.org

Runaways

Often there are situations in which teens feel they need to physically escape. Although many things can be dealt with over time, teens do run away. In such circumstances it is important they go to a safe place rather than staying on the streets.

National Runaway Switchboard	800-621-4000
National Runaway Hotline	800-231-6946

www.NRScrisisline.org
www.casayouthshelter.org

MODEL PROGRAM

Student Leadership Training

MODEL PROGRAM

The following is one example of a student leadership program that has proved to be immensely successful—Harvard-Westlake School's Peer Support Program. Obviously, this is only one example of the many possibilities for a successful student leadership program. It can be modified in various ways to fit specific logistics and needs.

At the end of each school year, sophomores are given the opportunity to apply to become peer support trainees during their junior year. The selection process requires that the applicants write about their personal experiences with peer support and the qualities that they feel would make them a good peer support leader. After interviews are held by the junior and senior coordinators (four juniors and four seniors), the group meets to select the sophomores to be trainees for the following school year. Ideally, for effective training, the size of the group should not exceed twenty-four, but clearly every program should form as appropriate.

At the beginning of the following year, the junior trainees and the senior leaders have a chance to get to know one another during a weekend retreat away from the school environment. Through a series of physical and mental challenges, the group develops teamwork and trust. By the end of the retreat, an incredibly strong bond has been created within the members of peer support.

Another integral part of the program is the relationship between the senior leaders and their junior trainees. Throughout the year, they work together—in our particular case we call it the Monday night program because we meet on Monday evenings. The senior leader acts as a mentor to the trainee, providing encouragement and guidance while the trainee learns the skills necessary to become an effective peer leader.

The foundation of the peer support program is based on effective training. Juniors are trained for an entire year during one class period per week, learning the basic communication skills. They are given the opportunity to truly develop and refine their skills for success as a peer support leader. Toward the end of the year, the juniors break up into simulated peer support groups to practice the communication skills in an actual situation and to develop a special bond with the "trainees."

In their senior year, they continue training during one class period per week. Their senior year is devoted to utilizing the communication skills, as well as focusing on more specific and advanced skills to help them to deal with common teen issues that may arise during the course of the year. Additionally, the seniors spend time debriefing what goes on in the Monday night groups. The purpose of the debrief is to ensure that the role of the leaders is being fulfilled within the group setting and that any problems that may arise are identified and dealt with as quickly as possible.

The Monday night peer support program is open to the entire high school. There are no limits on the number of members that the program will serve. Senior leaders serve as mentors to the junior trainees within each group. Ideally, each group has two senior leaders and two junior trainees. Groups meet formally once a week after school and discuss any issues, trivial or serious, that the group members have on their minds. Prior to the group meetings, refreshments are provided and members gather to socialize. This creates a greater sense of community among all of the participants in peer support.

Once in their small groups, maintaining a balance between the more serious, pressing issues and those that are not as urgent is vital. It is recommended that the groups have a maximum of ten people in order to maintain intimacy, to create a strong sense of trust, and to help establish a close-knit bond within the group.

The program also sponsors various all-school assemblies and presentations on significant issues within the school community. Recent assemblies have addressed such topics as acquaintance rape and alcohol abuse. In addition, leaders in the program venture out to conferences consisting of high schools and colleges with a variety of peer programs in order to explore the diverse programs existing throughout the state. As a result of their involvement in one of these conferences (in our case it was CAPP—California Association of Peer Programs), peer support leaders were inspired to develop a program called PARTI (Peer Awareness of Real Teen Issues) that addresses teenage issues through the presentation of various skits. The program is student written, directed, acted, and produced but certainly needs the continuing support and guidance of the peer support faculty advisor.

As active participants in peer support, our students have experienced firsthand the effects that their program has had on the community as well as on themselves. Through the training group, they have learned the essential communication skills that have helped them develop stronger relationships with friends and family. From their Monday night meetings, they developed close bonds with other students with whom they would otherwise never have been acquainted. The assemblies they sponsored and conferences they attended have made them more aware of the many issues teens are faced with, enabling them to reach out to their school community.

Finally, writing this workbook has helped us realize the value of communication skills and the impact that peer programs can have. We hope that you will take away the knowledge and passion that we have gained to help you realize the potential of peer programs.

The *Student Leadership Training* workbook is certainly a work in progress; therefore, we encourage feedback at any time to help keep this workbook accurate and up-to-date. Please feel free to e-mail your comments to: **dtaub@hw.com**

REFERENCES

The following materials have been helpful in writing this workbook.

Brackenbury, Cheryl. *Peer Helpers Plus*. Markham, Ontario: Pembroke, 1995.

Carr, Rey, and Saunders, Greg. *Peer Counselling Starter Kit*. Victoria, B.C.: Peer Systems Consulting Group, Inc., 1981.

The Community Board Program, Inc. 1987.

Myrick, Robert D., and Erney, Tom. *Caring and Sharing: Becoming a Peer Facilitator*. Minneapolis, Minn.: Educational Media Corporation, 1984.

Roberts, Gail. *Peer Counselor Workbook*. Victoria, B.C.: Peer Systems Consulting Group, Inc., 1998.

Tindall, Judith A. *Peer Power Book One*. Muncie, Ind.: Accelerated Development, 1989.

Tindall, Judith A. *Peer Power Book Two*. Muncie, Ind.: Accelerated Development, 1994.

Tindall, Judith A., and Salmon-White, Shirley. *Peers Helping Peers*. Muncie, Ind.: Accelerated Development, 1990.

ABOUT THE AUTHOR

Diane Taub's professional career spans over thirty years both in the United States and Canada. Extensive training in counseling and education, together with a solid foundation built from years of initiating and developing community-based programs, has made her a leader and sought-after authority on peer support.

As a mother of two children, Diane is motivated both personally and professionally. She has rounded out her training and experience with a number of positions that have prepared her as an outstanding facilitator and mentor. For most of her career, she was a guidance counselor at a variety of high schools, but she was also employed at York University and The University of Toronto as a Director of Counselor Education Courses, teaching human development, communication skills, and guidance. She has also taught Peer Support Training at UCLA.

Presently, Diane is Coordinator of Student Leadership Training at Harvard-Westlake School in Los Angeles. During the past four years she has developed the peer support program and has created the peer tutoring program.

She lives and works in Los Angeles with her husband, a television writer-producer, and makes frequent trips to Canada to visit her son in Vancouver and her daughter in Toronto. In addition to her busy work schedule, Diane finds time to nurture a serious passion for tennis, physical fitness, and travel.